Gordon Young

Preludes for Worship

Volume II

Original Organ Compositions

for Dr. D. DeWitt Wasson

If you enjoyed this collection please ask for Volume I, B-G0578.

FRED BOCK
PUBLISHING group

EXCLUSIVELY DISTRIBUTED BY

HAL•LEONARD®

7777 W. BLUEMOUND RD. P.O. BOX 13819 MILWAUKEE, WI 53213

BAROQUE TRUMPET

Sw. Foundations
Gt. Trumpet 8′
Ped. 16′ to Sw.

Gordon Young

B-G0672

4

CATHEDRAL FANFARE
(After Agincourt)

Full Organ

Gordon Young

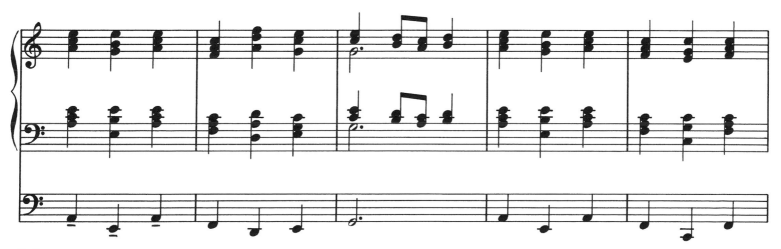

B-G0672

simile

NOEL
(With Variations)

Sw. Solo reed 8'
Gt. Foundations
Ch. Flutes
Ped. 16' to Ch.

Gordon Young

B-G0672

BACHIANA ON AN ANCIENT CHORALE

Full Organ

Gordon Young

B-G0672

RIGAUDON

Full Organ

Gordon Young

MUSETTE

Sw. Reed 8′
Ch. 8′, 2′
Ped. 16′ to Ch.

Gordon Young

B-G0672

PSALM XXIII
(Green Pastures)

Sw. Flutes
Gt. 8', 4'
Ch. Cromorne 8'
Ped. 16' to Sw.

Gordon Young

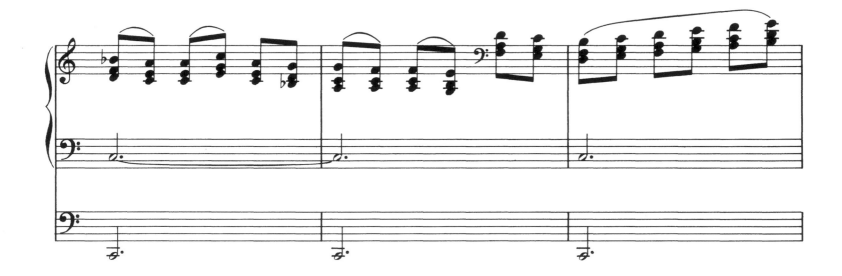

B-G0672

CLASSIC TRIO

Sw. Solo stop
Gt. Light Foundations
Ch. 8', 2'
Ped. 16' to Ch.

Gordon Young

B-G0672

YORKMINSTER PROCESSIONAL

Full Combinations

Gordon Young

B-G0672